ABOUT ME

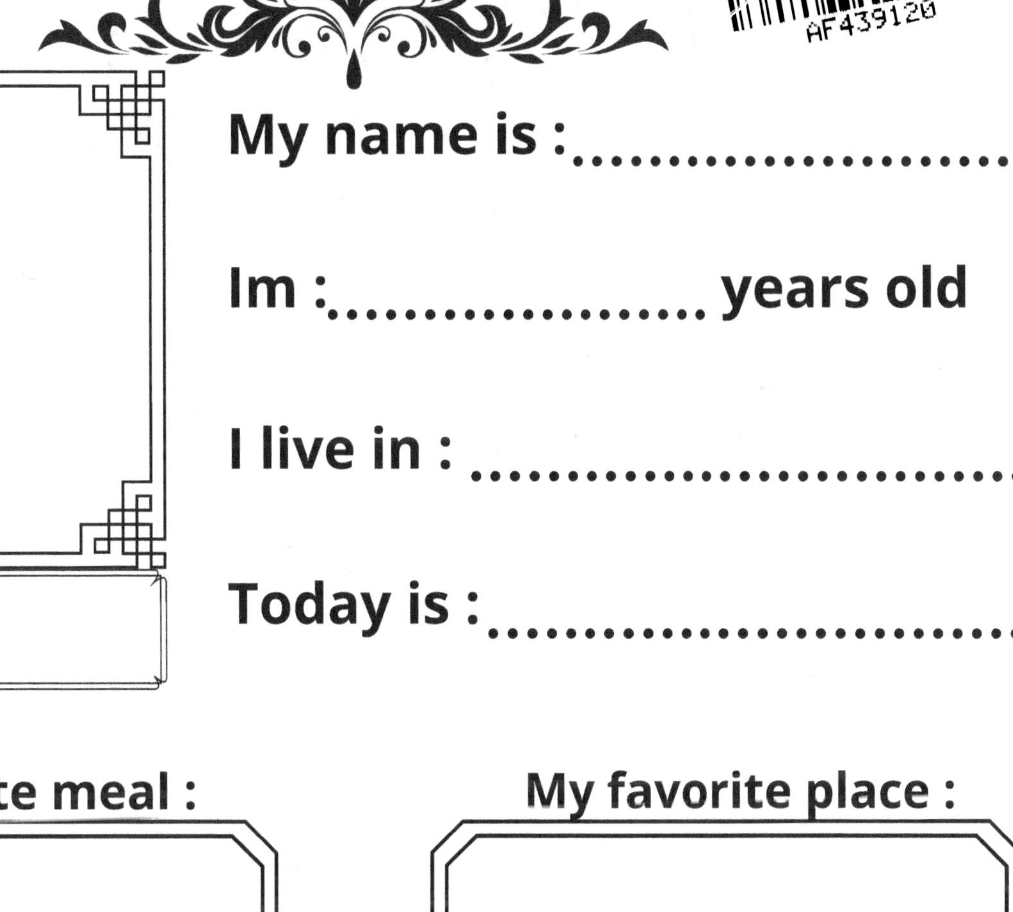

My name is :.........................

Im :.................... years old

I live in : ....

Today is :..............................

Me

My favorite meal :

My favorite place :

My favorite book:

My favorite sport :

رمضان كريم
Countdown to Eid!
1 2 3 4 5
6 7 8 9 10
11 12 13 14 15
16 17 18 19 20
21 22 23 24 25
26 27 28 29 30

PILLARS OF ISLAM

عن عبدالله بن عمر رضي الله عنهما قال: سمعت رسول الله ﷺ يقولُ: ((بُنِي الإسلامُ عَلى خَمْسٍ: شَهادةِ أنْ لا إلهَ إلاَّ الله، وأنَّ مُحمَّداً عَبْدُه وَرَسولُهُ، وإقامِ الصلاةِ، وإيتاءِ الزَّكاةِ، وحَجِّ البيتِ، وصَومِ رَمضانَ))

رواهُ البُخارَي ومُسلمٌ

THE MESSENGER OF ALLAH (ﷺ) SAID, "(THE STRUCTURE OF) ISLAM IS BUILT ON FIVE (PILLARS): TESTIFICATION OF 'LA ILAHA ILLALLAH' (NONE HAS THE RIGHT TO BE WORSHIPPED BUT ALLAH), THAT MUHAMMAD (ﷺ) IS HIS SLAVE AND MESSENGER, THE ESTABLISHMENT OF SALAT, THE PAYMENT OF ZAKAT, THE PILGRIMAGE TO THE HOUSE OF ALLAH (KA'BAH), AND SAUM DURING THE MONTH OF RAMADAN."

Narrated by Al-Bukhaari and Muslim

ADHAN
call to prayer

Allah Akbar , Allah 'Akbar ,

Allah 'Akbar , Allah 'Akbar

Ashhad 'an la 'iilah 'iila allah ,

Ashhad 'an la 'iilah 'iila allah

Ashhad 'ana Muhamadan rasul allah ,

Ashhad 'ana Muhamadan rasul allah

Haya ealaa al Salat ,

Haya ealaa al Salat

Haya ealaa al Falah

Haya ealaa al Falah

Allah 'Akbar , Allah 'Akbar

la 'iilah 'iila allah

SALAH
prayer

To pray five times each day ...

Fajr ◄······► Before Sunrise

Zuhr ◄······► Early Afternoon

Asr ◄······► Late afternon

Maghrib ◄···► After Sunset

Isha ◄······► Night

رمضان كريم

كل عام وانتم بخير

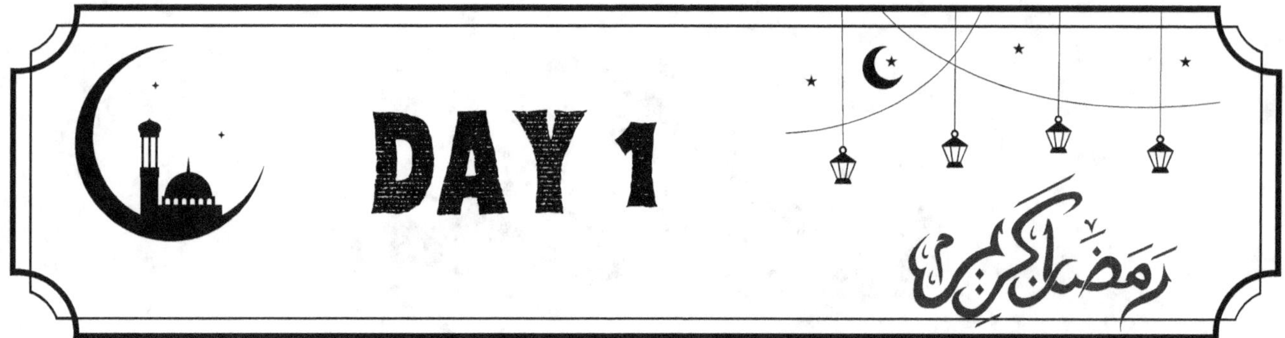

color a flag for every prayer you made

FAJR	ZUHR	ASR	MAGHRIB	ISHA
2	4	4	3	4

My goal for to day

....

....

....

Healthy Habits

WATER:

EXERCISE: _ _ _ _ _ _ _ _ _ _ _

MOOD:

My good dees

I read quran ☐

I did zikr ☐

I gavr sadaqah ☐

choosenan ayah to copy here

بِسْمِ اللَّهِ الرَّحْمَنِ الرَّحِيمِ

Dua of The Day

رَبَّنَا لاَ تُؤَاخِذْنَا إِن نَّسِينَا أَوْ أَخْطَأْنَا

RABBANA LAA TU'AAKHIZNAAA IN NASEENAAA AW AKHTAANAA

"OUR LORD, DO NOT IMPOSE BLAME UPON US IF WE HAVE FORGOTTEN OR ERRED."
– 2:286 –

Reflections of The Day

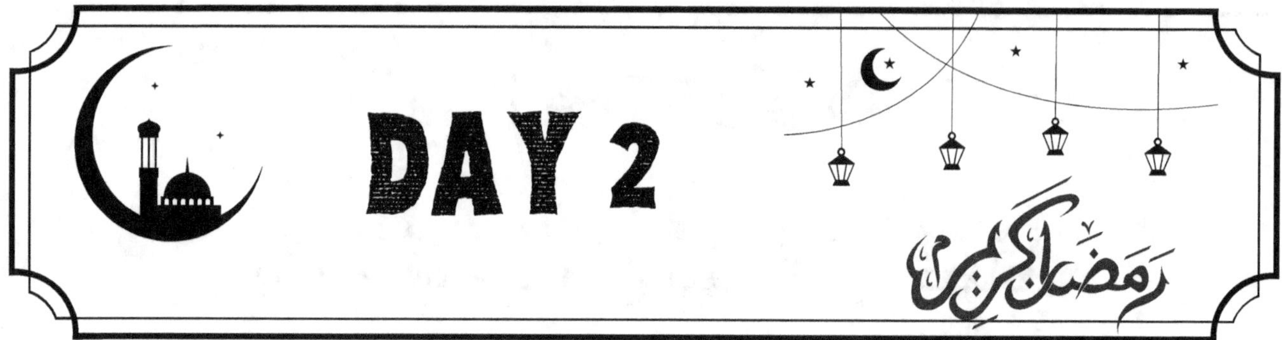

color a flag for every prayer you made

FAJR	ZUHR	ASR	MAGHRIB	ISHA
2	4	4	3	4

My goal for to day

....

....

....

choosenan ayah to copy here

بِسْمِ اللهِ الرَّحْمَنِ الرَّحِيمِ

....

....

....

....

....

....

Healthy Habits

WATER:

EXERCISE: _ _ _ _ _ _ _ _ _ _ _

MOOD:

My good dees

I read quran ☐

I did zikr ☐

I gavr sadaqah ☐

Dua of The Day

رَبَّنَا وَلَا تُحَمِّلْنَا مَا لَا طَاقَةَ لَنَا بِهِ

RABBANA WALA TUHAMMILNA MA LA TAQATA LANA BIHI

OUR LORD, DO NOT IMPOSE ON US MORE THAN WE HAVE THE STRENGTH TO BEAR
– 2:286 –

Reflections of The Day

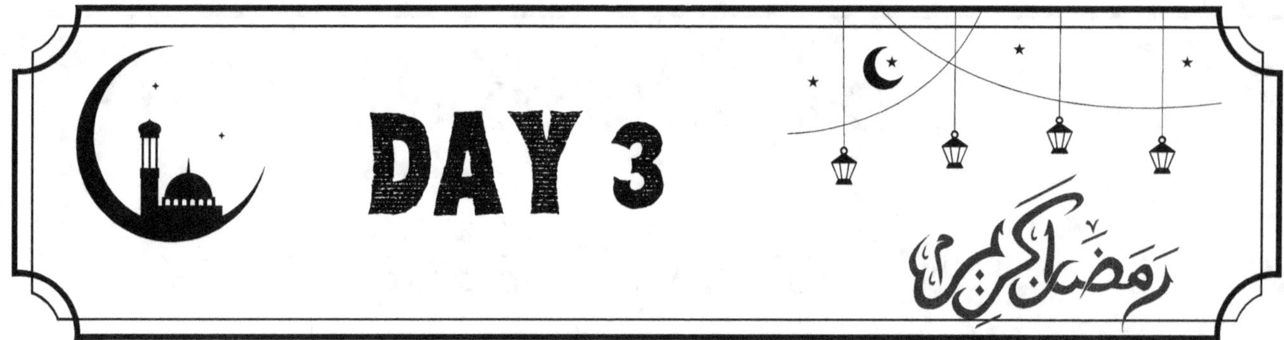

color a flag for every prayer you made

FAJR	ZUHR	ASR	MAGHRIB	ISHA
2	4	4	3	4

My goal for to day

....
....
....

Healthy Habits

WATER:

EXERCISE: _ _ _ _ _ _ _ _ _ _

MOOD:

My good dees

I read quran ☐

I did zikr ☐

I gavr sadaqah ☐

choosenan ayah to copy here

بِسْمِ اللهِ الرَّحْمَنِ الرَّحِيمِ

Dua of The Day

رَبَّنَا أَفْرِغْ عَلَيْنَا صَبْراً وَثَبِّتْ أَقْدَامَنَا وَانصُرْنَا عَلَى القَوْمِ الكَافِرِينَ

RABBANA AFRIGH 'ALAINAA SABRAN WA SABBIT AQDAAMANAA WANSURNAA 'ALAL QAWMIL KAAFIREEN

"OUR LORD, POUR UPON US PATIENCE AND PLANT FIRMLY OUR FEET AND GIVE US VICTORY OVER THE DISBELIEVING PEOPLE."
– 2:250 –

Reflections of The Day

____

____

____

____

____

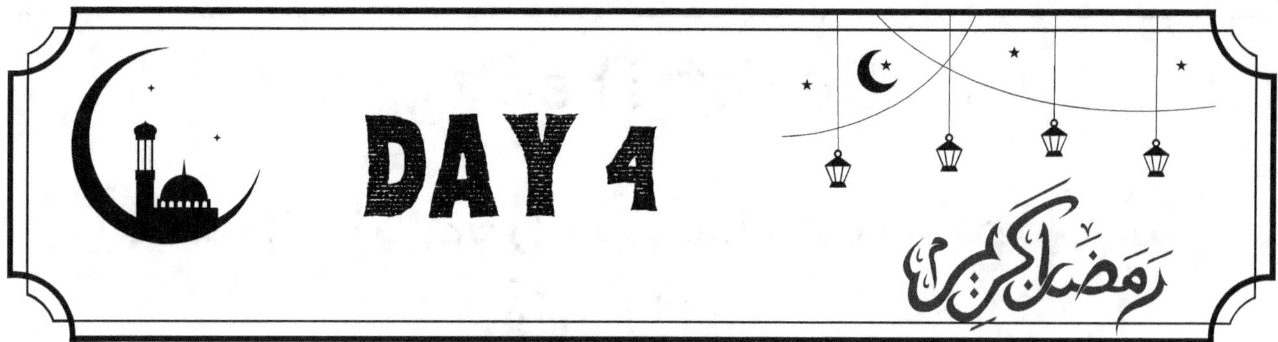

color a flag for every prayer you made

FAJR	ZUHR	ASR	MAGHRIB	ISHA
2	4	4	3	4

My goal for to day

....
....
....

Healthy Habits

WATER:

EXERCISE: ___________

MOOD:

My good dees

I read quran ☐

I did zikr ☐

I gavr sadaqah ☐

choosenan ayah to copy here

بِسْمِ اللهِ الرَّحْمَنِ الرَّحِيمِ

Dua of The Day

رَبَّنَا وَلاَ تَحْمِلْ عَلَيْنَا إِصْرًا كَمَا حَمَلْتَهُ عَلَى الَّذِينَ مِن قَبْلِنَا

RABBANA WA LAA TAHMIL-'ALAINAAA ISRAN KAMAA HAMALTAHOO 'ALAL-LAZEENA MIN QABLINAA

"OUR LORD, AND LAY NOT UPON US A BURDEN LIKE THAT WHICH YOU LAID UPON THOSE BEFORE US."
– 2:286 –

Reflections of The Day

____

____

____

____

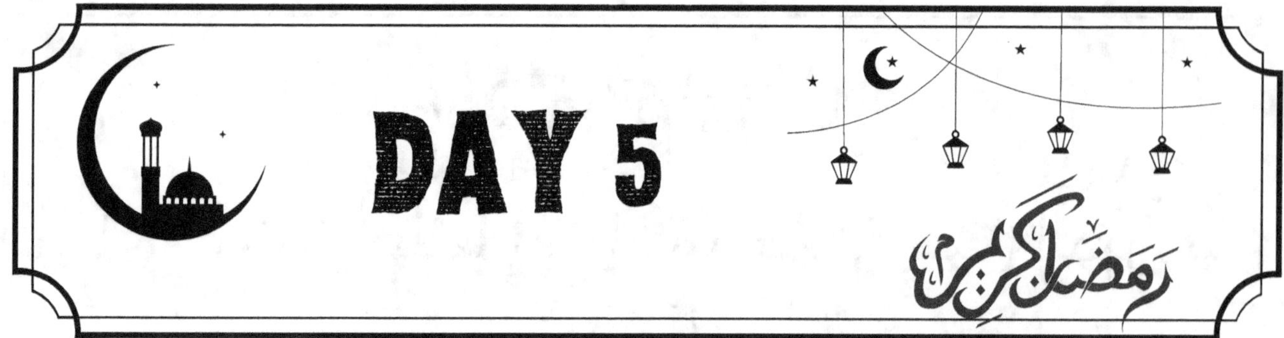

color a flag for every prayer you made

FAJR	ZUHR	ASR	MAGHRIB	ISHA
2	4	4	3	4

My goal for to day

Healthy Habits

WATER:

EXERCISE: _ _ _ _ _ _ _ _ _ _

MOOD:

My good dees

I read quran ☐

I did zikr ☐

I gavr sadaqah ☐

choosenan ayah to copy here

Dua of The Day

رَبَّنَا لاَ تُزِغْ قُلُوبَنَا بَعْدَ إِذْ هَدَيْتَنَا وَهَبْ لَنَا مِن لَّدُنكَ رَحْمَةً إِنَّكَ أَنتَ الْوَهَّابُ

RABBANA LAA TUZIGH QULOOBANAA BA'DA IZ HADAITANAA WA HAB LANAA MIL LADUNKA RAHMAH; INNAKA ANTAL WAHHAAB

"OUR LORD, LET NOT OUR HEARTS DEVIATE AFTER YOU HAVE GUIDED US AND GRANT US FROM YOURSELF MERCY. INDEED, YOU ARE THE BESTOWER."

– 3:8 –

Reflections of The Day

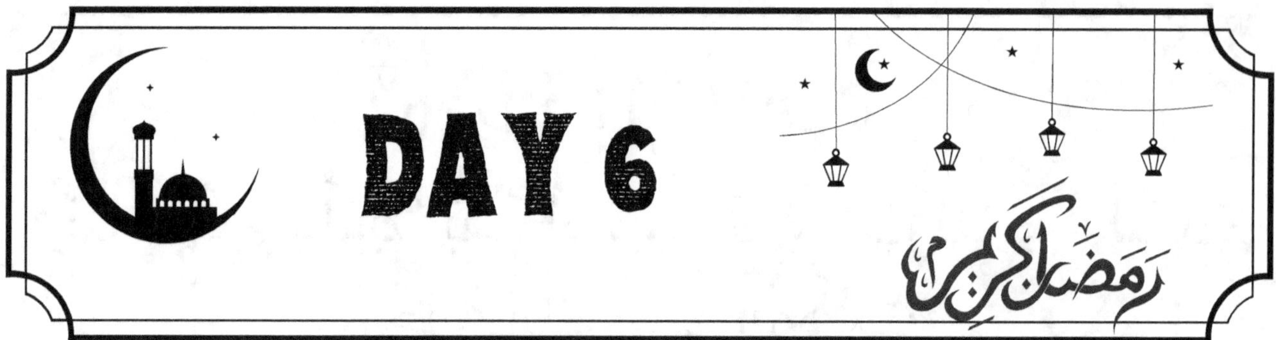

DAY 6

color a flag for every prayer you made

FAJR	ZUHR	ASR	MAGHRIB	ISHA
2	4	4	3	4

My goal for to day

....
....
....

Healthy Habits

WATER:

EXERCISE: _ _ _ _ _ _ _ _ _ _ _

MOOD:

My good dees

I read quran ☐

I did zikr ☐

I gavr sadaqah ☐

choosenan ayah to copy here

بِسْمِ اللهِ الرَّحْمَنِ الرَّحِيمِ

Dua of The Day

رَبَّنَا إِنَّكَ جَامِعُ النَّاسِ لِيَوْمٍ لاَّ رَيْبَ فِيهِ إِنَّ اللّهَ لاَ يُخْلِفُ الْمِيعَادَ

RABBANA INNAKA JAMI'UNNASI LI-YAWMIL LA RAIBA FI INNALLAHA LA YUKHLIFUL MI'AAD

"OUR LORD, SURELY YOU WILL GATHER THE PEOPLE FOR A DAY ABOUT WHICH THERE IS NO DOUBT. INDEED, ALLAH DOES NOT FAIL IN HIS PROMISE."

– 3:9 –

Reflections of The Day

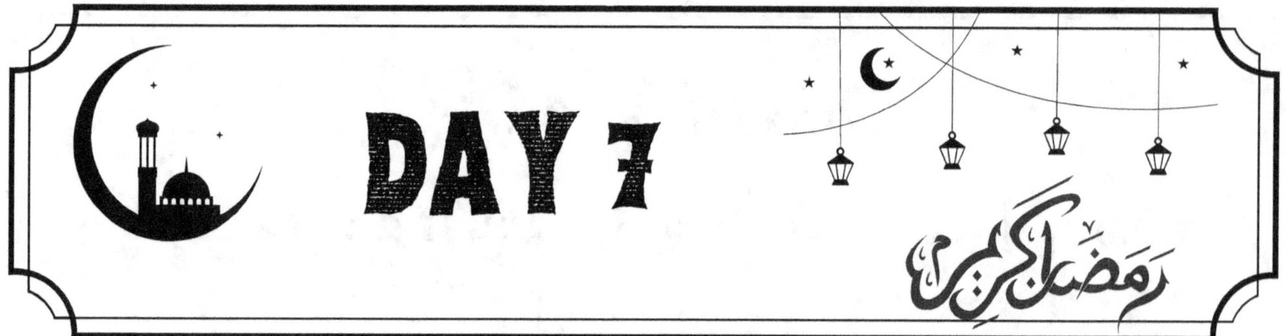

color a flag for every prayer you made

FAJR	ZUHR	ASR	MAGHRIB	ISHA
2	4	4	3	4

My goal for to day

....
....
....

Healthy Habits

WATER:

EXERCISE: _ _ _ _ _ _ _ _ _ _

MOOD:

My good dees

I read quran ☐

I did zikr ☐

I gavr sadaqah ☐

choosenan ayah to copy here

بِسْمِ اللهِ الرَّحْمَنِ الرَّحِيمِ

Dua of The Day

رَبَّنَا إِنَّنَا آمَنَّا فَاغْفِرْ لَنَا ذُنُوبَنَا وَقِنَا عَذَابَ النَّارِ

**RABBANAAA INNANAAA AAMANNAA FAGHFIR LANAA ZUNOOBANAA
WA QINAA 'AZAABAN NAAR**

**"OUR LORD, INDEED WE HAVE BELIEVED, SO FORGIVE US OUR SINS
AND PROTECT US FROM THE PUNISHMENT OF THE FIRE"
– 3:16 –**

Reflections of The Day

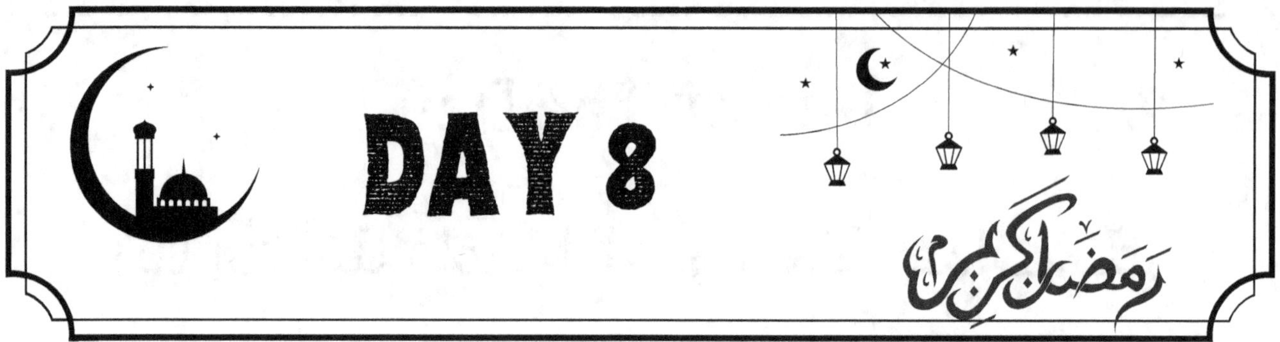

DAY 8

color a flag for every prayer you made

FAJR	ZUHR	ASR	MAGHRIB	ISHA
2	4	4	3	4

My goal for to day

....
....
....

choosenan ayah to copy here

بِسْمِ اللَّهِ الرَّحْمَٰنِ الرَّحِيمِ

Healthy Habits

WATER:

EXERCISE: _ _ _ _ _ _ _ _ _ _

MOOD:

My good dees

I read quran ☐

I did zikr ☐

I gavr sadaqah ☐

Dua of The Day

رَبَّنَآ عَامَنَّا بِمَآ أَنزَلْتَ وَٱتَّبَعْنَا ٱلرَّسُولَ فَٱكْتُبْنَا مَعَ ٱلشِّهِدِينَ

RABBANAAA AAMANNAA BIMAAA ANZALTA WATTABA'NAR RASOOLA FAKTUBNAA MA'ASH SHAAHIDEEN

"OUR LORD, WE HAVE BELIEVED IN WHAT YOU REVEALED AND HAVE FOLLOWED THE MESSENGER, SO REGISTER US AMONG THE WITNESSES [TO TRUTH]."
– 3:53 –

Reflections of The Day

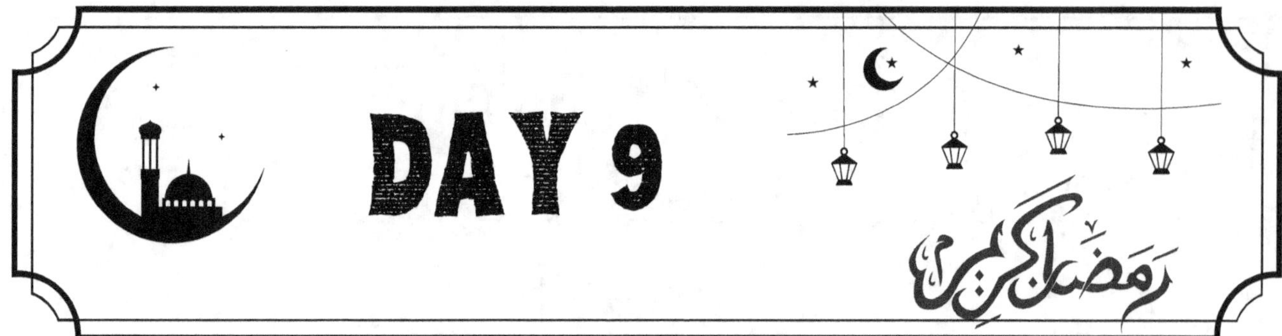

color a flag for every prayer you made

FAJR	ZUHR	ASR	MAGHRIB	ISHA
2	4	4	3	4

My goal for to day

....

....

....

Healthy Habits

WATER:

EXERCISE: _ _ _ _ _ _ _ _ _ _ _

MOOD:

My good dees

I read quran ☐

I did zikr ☐

I gavr sadaqah ☐

choosenan ayah to copy here

بِسْمِ اللهِ الرَّحْمٰنِ الرَّحِيمِ

Dua of The Day

رَبَّنَا اغْفِرْ لَنَا ذُنُوبَنَا وَإِسْرَافَنَا فِي أَمْرِنَا وَثَبِّتْ أَقْدَامَنَا وانصُرْنَا عَلَى الْقَوْمِ الْكَافِرِينَ

RABBANAGH FIR LANAA ZUNOOBANAA WA ISRAAFANAA FEEE AMIRNAA WA SABBIT AQDAAMANAA WANSURNAA 'ALAL QAWMIL KAAFIREEN

"OUR LORD, FORGIVE US OUR SINS AND THE EXCESS [COMMITTED] IN OUR AFFAIRS AND PLANT FIRMLY OUR FEET AND GIVE US VICTORY OVER THE DISBELIEVING PEOPLE."

– 3:147 –

Reflections of The Day

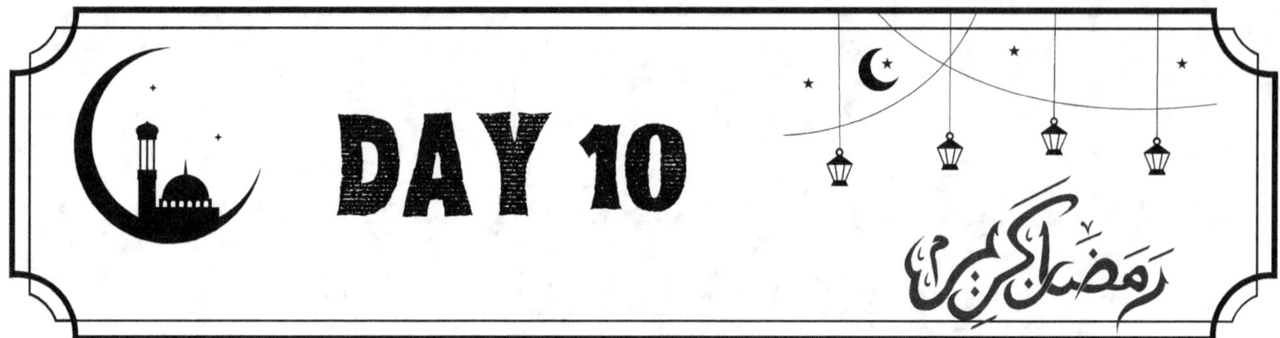

color a flag for every prayer you made

FAJR	ZUHR	ASR	MAGHRIB	ISHA
2	4	4	3	4

My goal for to day

....
....
....

Healthy Habits

WATER:

EXERCISE: _ _ _ _ _ _ _ _ _ _ _

MOOD:

My good dees

I read quran ☐

I did zikr ☐

I gavr sadaqah ☐

choosenan ayah to copy here

بِسْمِ اللهِ الرَّحْمٰنِ الرَّحِيمِ

....
....
....
....
....
....

Dua of The Day

رَبَّنَا مَا خَلَقْتَ هَذا بَاطِلاً سُبْحَانَكَ فَقِنَا عَذَابَ النَّارِ

RABBANAA MAA KHALAQTA HAAZA BAATILAN SUBHAANAKA FAQINAA 'AZAABAN NAAR

"OUR LORD, YOU DID NOT CREATE THIS AIMLESSLY; EXALTED ARE YOU [ABOVE SUCH A THING]; THEN PROTECT US FROM THE PUNISHMENT OF THE FIRE."
– 3:191 –

Reflections of The Day

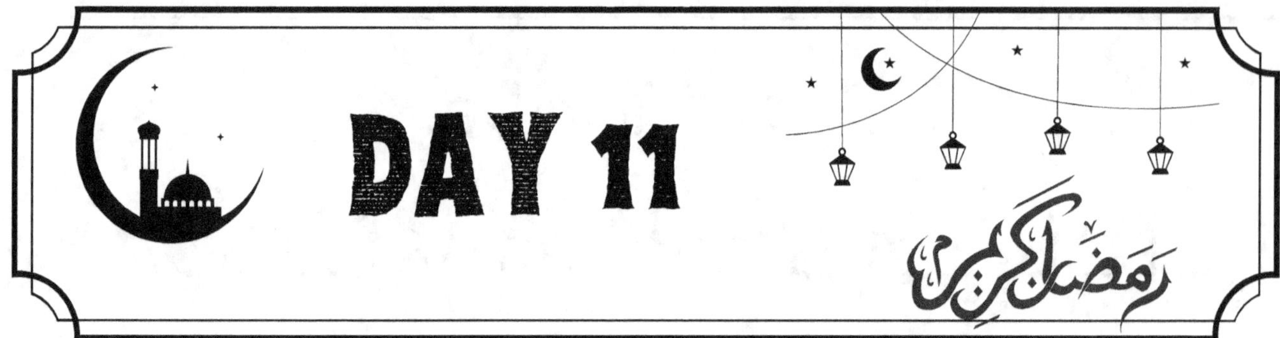

DAY 11

color a flag for every prayer you made

FAJR	ZUHR	ASR	MAGHRIB	ISHA
2	4	4	3	4

My goal for to day

....
....
....

Healthy Habits

WATER:

EXERCISE: _ _ _ _ _ _ _ _ _ _ _

MOOD:

My good dees

I read quran ☐

I did zikr ☐

I gavr sadaqah ☐

choosenan ayah to copy here

بِسْمِ اللّٰهِ الرَّحْمٰنِ الرَّحِيمِ
....
....
....
....
....
....

Dua of The Day

رَبَّنَا فَاغْفِرْ لَنَا ذُنُوبَنَا وَكَفِّرْ عَنَّا سَيِّئَاتِنَا وَتَوَفَّنَا مَعَ الأبْرَارِ

RABBANAA FAGHFIR LANAA ZUNOOBANAA WA KAFFIR 'ANNAA SAIYI AATINA WA TAWAFFANAA MA'AL ABRAAR

"OUR LORD, SO FORGIVE US OUR SINS AND REMOVE FROM US OUR MISDEEDS AND CAUSE US TO DIE AMONG THE RIGHTEOUS."

– 3:193 –

Reflections of The Day

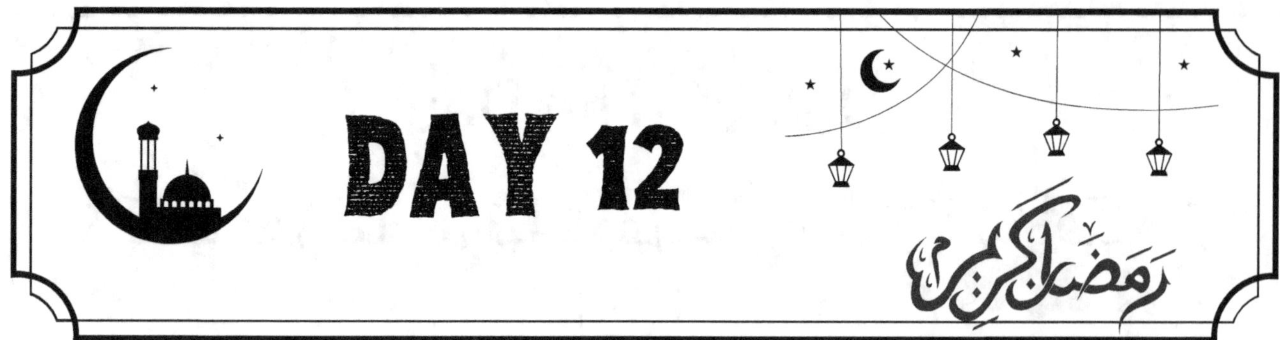

color a flag for every prayer you made

FAJR	ZUHR	ASR	MAGHRIB	ISHA
2	4	4	3	4

My goal for to day

....

....

....

Healthy Habits

WATER:

EXERCISE: _ _ _ _ _ _ _ _ _ _

MOOD:

My good dees

I read quran ☐

I did zikr ☐

I gavr sadaqah ☐

choosenan ayah to copy here

بِسْمِ اللهِ الرَّحْمَنِ الرَّحِيمِ

Dua of The Day

رَّبَّنَا إِنَّنَا سَمِعْنَا مُنَادِيًا يُنَادِي لِلإِيمَانِ أَنْ آمِنُواْ بِرَبِّكُمْ فَآمَنَّا

RABBANAAA INNANAA SAMI'NAA MUNAADIYAI YUNAADEE LIL
EEMAANI AN AAMINOO BI RABBIKUM FA AAMANNAA

"OUR LORD, INDEED WE HAVE HEARD A CALLER, CALLING TO FAITH,
[SAYING], 'BELIEVE IN YOUR LORD,' AND WE HAVE BELIEVED."
– 3:193 –

Reflections of The Day

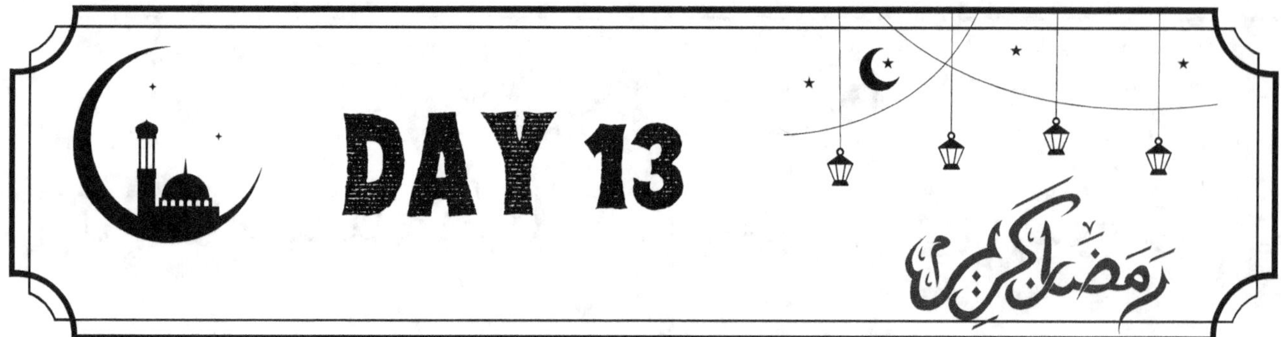

color a flag for every prayer you made

FAJR	ZUHR	ASR	MAGHRIB	ISHA
2	4	4	3	4

My goal for to day

....

....

....

Healthy Habits

WATER:

EXERCISE: _ _ _ _ _ _ _ _ _ _

MOOD:

My good dees

I read quran ☐

I did zikr ☐

I gavr sadaqah ☐

choosenan ayah to copy here

بِسْمِ اللهِ الرَّحْمَنِ الرَّحِيمِ

Dua of The Day

رَبَّنَا آمَنَّا فَاكْتُبْنَا مَعَ الشَّاهِدِينَ

RABBANA AAMANA FAKTUBNA MA' ASH-SHAHIDEEN

"OUR LORD, WE HAVE BELIEVED, SO REGISTER US AMONG THE WITNESSES."
– 5:83 –

Reflections of The Day

____

____

____

____

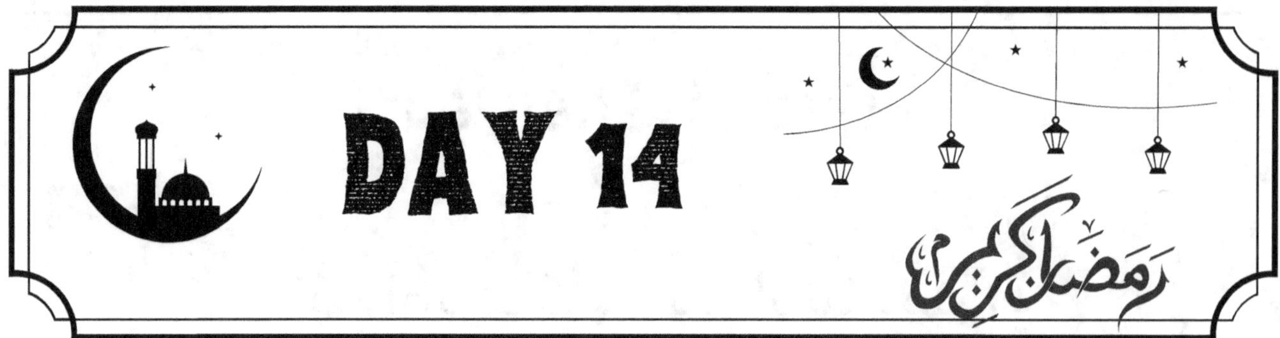

color a flag for every prayer you made

FAJR	ZUHR	ASR	MAGHRIB	ISHA
2	4	4	3	4

My goal for to day

....

....

....

choosenan ayah to copy here

Healthy Habits

WATER:

EXERCISE: _ _ _ _ _ _ _ _ _ _

MOOD:

My good dees

I read quran ☐

I did zikr ☐

I gavr sadaqah ☐

Dua of The Day

رَبَّنَا ظَلَمْنَا أَنفُسَنَا وَإِن لَّمْ تَغْفِرْ لَنَا وَتَرْحَمْنَا لَنَكُونَنَّ مِنَ الْخَاسِرِينَ

RABBANA ZALAMNA ANFUSINA WA IL LAM TAGHFIR LANA WA TARHAMNA LANAKOONANNA MINAL KHAASIREEN

"OUR LORD, WE HAVE WRONGED OURSELVES, AND IF YOU DO NOT FORGIVE US AND HAVE MERCY UPON US, WE WILL SURELY BE AMONG THE LOSERS."
– 7:23 –

Reflections of The Day

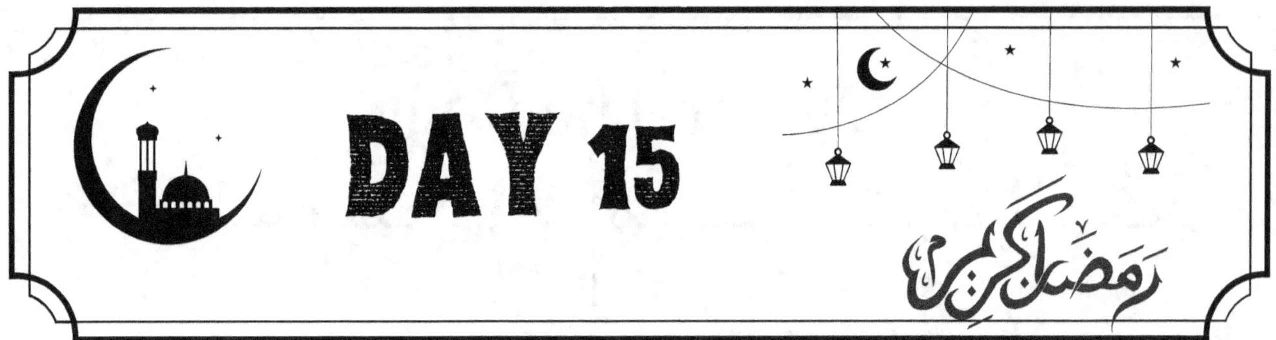

color a flag for every prayer you made

FAJR	ZUHR	ASR	MAGHRIB	ISHA
2	4	4	3	4

My goal for to day

....
....
....

choosenan ayah to copy here

Healthy Habits

WATER:

EXERCISE: _ _ _ _ _ _ _ _ _ _

MOOD:

My good dees

I read quran ☐

I did zikr ☐

I gavr sadaqah ☐

Dua of The Day

رَبَّنَا لاَ تَجْعَلْنَا مَعَ الْقَوْمِ الظَّالِمِينَ

RABBANA LA TAJ'ALNA MA'AL QAWWMI-DHALIMEEN

"OUR LORD, DO NOT PLACE US WITH THE WRONGDOING PEOPLE."
– 7:47 –

Reflections of The Day

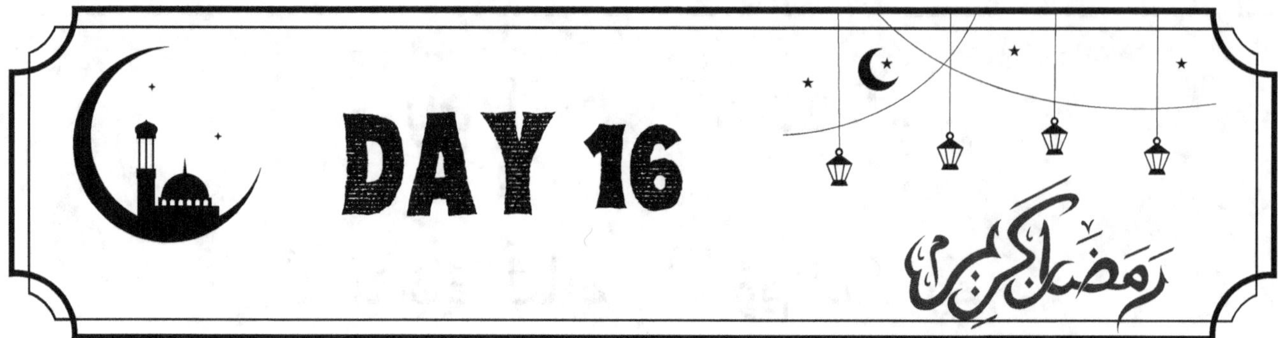

color a flag for every prayer you made

FAJR	ZUHR	ASR	MAGHRIB	ISHA
2	4	4	3	4

My goal for to day

....

....

....

Healthy Habits

WATER:

EXERCISE: _ _ _ _ _ _ _ _ _ _

MOOD:

My good dees

I read quran ☐

I did zikr ☐

I gavr sadaqah ☐

choosenan ayah to copy here

بِسْمِ اللهِ الرَّحْمٰنِ الرَّحِيمِ

....

....

....

....

....

....

Dua of The Day

رَبَّنَا افْتَحْ بَيْنَنَا وَبَيْنَ قَوْمِنَا بِالْحَقِّ وَأَنتَ خَيْرُ الْفَاتِحِينَ

RABBANAF-TAH BAINANA WA BAINA QAWMINA BIL HAQQI WA ANTA KHAIRUL FATIHEEN

"OUR LORD, DECIDE BETWEEN US AND OUR PEOPLE IN TRUTH, AND YOU ARE THE BEST OF THOSE WHO GIVE DECISION."
– 7:89 –

Reflections of The Day

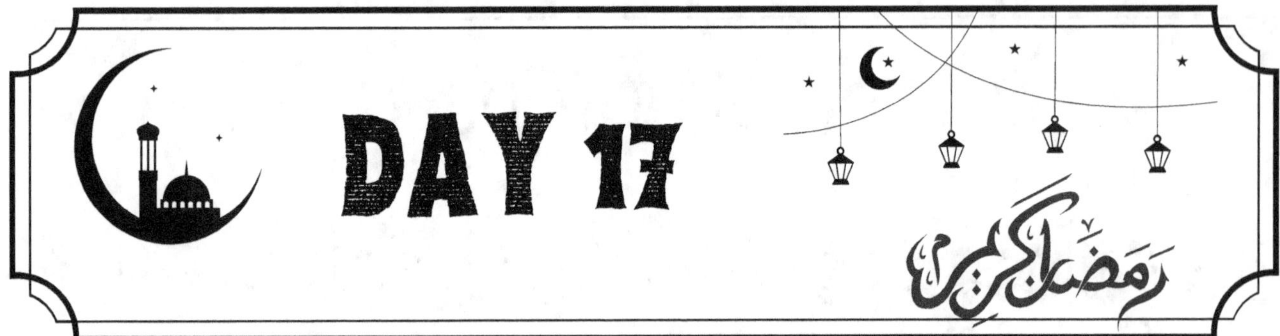

color a flag for every prayer you made

FAJR	ZUHR	ASR	MAGHRIB	ISHA
2	4	4	3	4

My goal for to day

....
....
....

choosenan ayah to copy here

بِسْمِ اللهِ الرَّحْمَنِ الرَّحِيمِ

Healthy Habits

WATER:

EXERCISE: _ _ _ _ _ _ _ _ _ _

MOOD:

My good dees

I read quran ☐

I did zikr ☐

I gavr sadaqah ☐

Dua of The Day

رَبَّنَا أَفْرِغْ عَلَيْنَا صَبْرًا وَتَوَفَّنَا مُسْلِمِينَ

RABBANA AFRIGH 'ALAINA SABRAW WA TAWAFFANA MUSLIMEEN

**"OUR LORD, POUR UPON US PATIENCE AND LET US DIE AS MUSLIMS
[IN SUBMISSION TO YOU]."**
– 7:126 –

Reflections of The Day

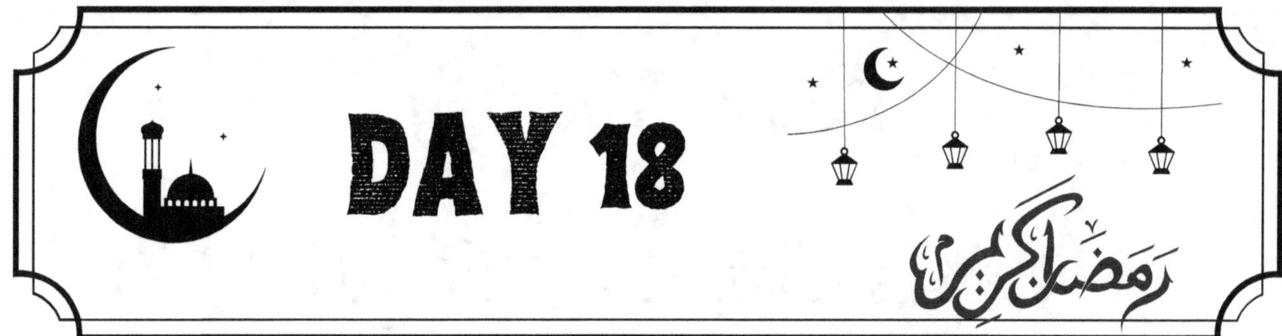

color a flag for every prayer you made

FAJR	ZUHR	ASR	MAGHRIB	ISHA
2	4	4	3	4

My goal for to day

....
....
....

Healthy Habits

WATER:

EXERCISE: _ _ _ _ _ _ _ _ _ _

MOOD:

My good dees

I read quran ☐

I did zikr ☐

I gavr sadaqah ☐

choosenan ayah to copy here

بِسْمِ اللَّهِ الرَّحْمَٰنِ الرَّحِيمِ

....
....
....
....
....
....

Dua of The Day

رَبَّنَا لاَ تَجْعَلْنَا فِتْنَةً لِّلْقَوْمِ الظَّالِمِينَ ؛ وَنَجِّنَا بِرَحْمَتِكَ مِنَ الْقَوْمِ الْكَافِرِينَ

85. RABBANA LA TAJ'ALNA FITNATAL LIL-QAWMIDH-DHALIMEEN ; 86. WA NAJJINA BI- RAHMATIKA MINAL QAWMIL KAFIREEN

"OUR LORD, MAKE US NOT [OBJECTS OF] TRIAL FOR THE WRONGDOING PEOPLE. AND SAVE US BY YOUR MERCY FROM THE DISBELIEVING PEOPLE."
– 10:85-86 –

Reflections of The Day

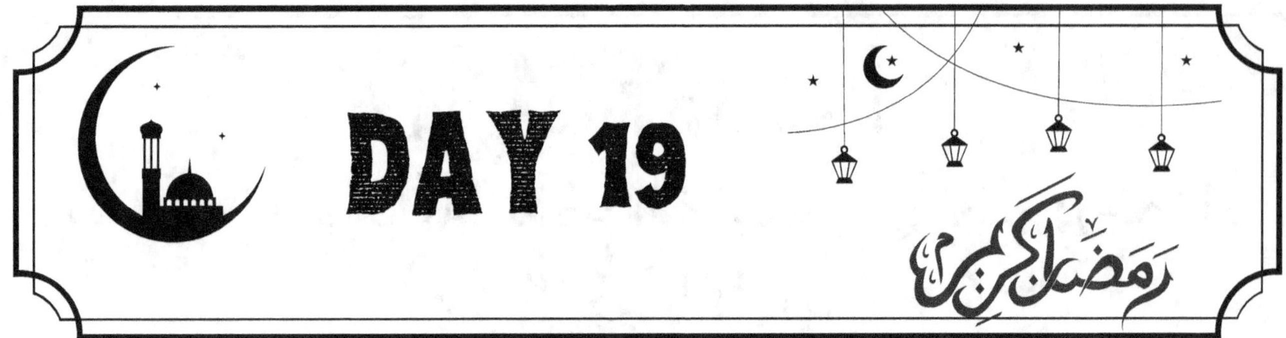

color a flag for every prayer you made

FAJR	ZUHR	ASR	MAGHRIB	ISHA
2	4	4	3	4

My goal for to day

....
....
....

choosenan ayah to copy here

بِسْمِ اللَّهِ الرَّحْمَٰنِ الرَّحِيمِ

Healthy Habits

WATER:

EXERCISE: _ _ _ _ _ _ _ _ _ _

MOOD:

My good dees

I read quran ☐

I did zikr ☐

I gavr sadaqah ☐

Dua of The Day

رَبِّ اجْعَلْنِي مُقِيمَ الصَّلَاةِ وَمِنْ ذُرِّيَّتِي رَبَّنَا وَتَقَبَّلْ دُعَاءِ

RABBIJ 'ALNEE MUQEEMAS SALAATI WA MIN ZURRIYYATEE RABBANAA WA TAQABBAL DU'AAA

"MY LORD, MAKE ME AN ESTABLISHER OF PRAYER, AND [MANY] FROM MY DESCENDANTS. OUR LORD, AND ACCEPT MY SUPPLICATION."

– 14:40 –

Reflections of The Day

____

____

____

____

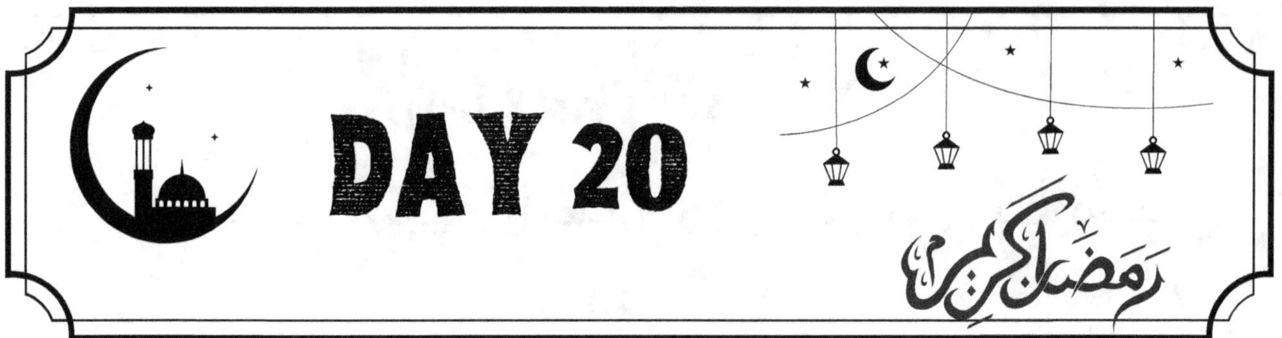

color a flag for every prayer you made

FAJR **ZUHR** **ASR** **MAGHRIB** **ISHA**

2 4 4 3 4

My goal for to day

....
....
....

choosenan ayah to copy here

Healthy Habits

WATER:

EXERCISE: _ _ _ _ _ _ _ _ _ _

MOOD:

My good dees

I read quran ☐

I did zikr ☐

I gavr sadaqah ☐

Dua of The Day

رَبَّنَا اغْفِرْ لِي وَلِوَالِدَيَّ وَلِلْمُؤْمِنِينَ يَوْمَ يَقُومُ الْحِسَابُ

RABBANAGH FIR LEE WA LIWAALIDAIYA WA LILMU'MINEENA YAWMA YAQOOMUL HISAAB

"OUR LORD, FORGIVE ME AND MY PARENTS AND THE BELIEVERS THE DAY THE ACCOUNT IS ESTABLISHED."
– 14:41 –

Reflections of The Day

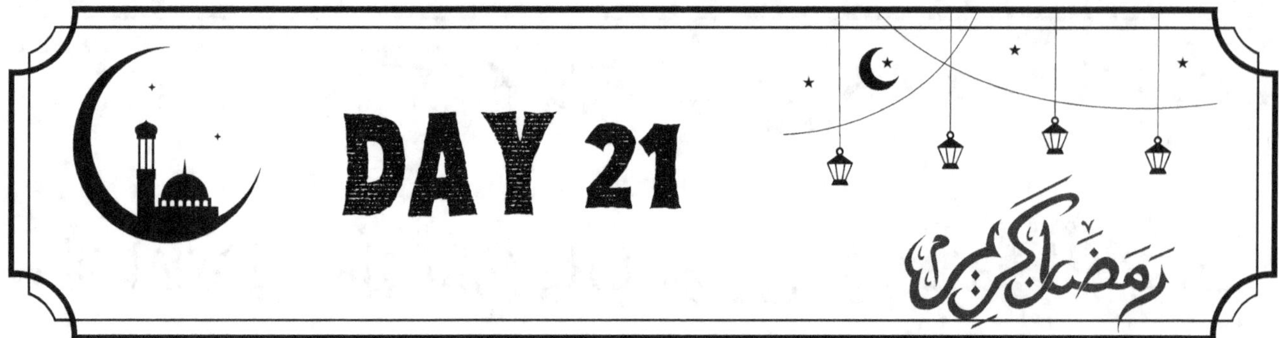

color a flag for every prayer you made

FAJR	ZUHR	ASR	MAGHRIB	ISHA
2	4	4	3	4

My goal for to day

Healthy Habits

WATER:

EXERCISE: _ _ _ _ _ _ _ _ _ _

MOOD:

My good dees

I read quran ☐

I did zikr ☐

I gavr sadaqah ☐

choosenan ayah to copy here

Dua of The Day

رَبَّنَا إِنَّنَا نَخَافُ أَن يَفْرُطَ عَلَيْنَا أَوْ أَن يَطْغَى

RABBANA INNANA NAKHAFU AI-YAFRUTA 'ALAINA AW ANY-YATGHA

"OUR LORD, INDEED WE ARE AFRAID THAT HE WILL HASTEN [PUNISHMENT] AGAINST US OR THAT HE WILL TRANSGRESS."
– 20:45 –

Reflections of The Day

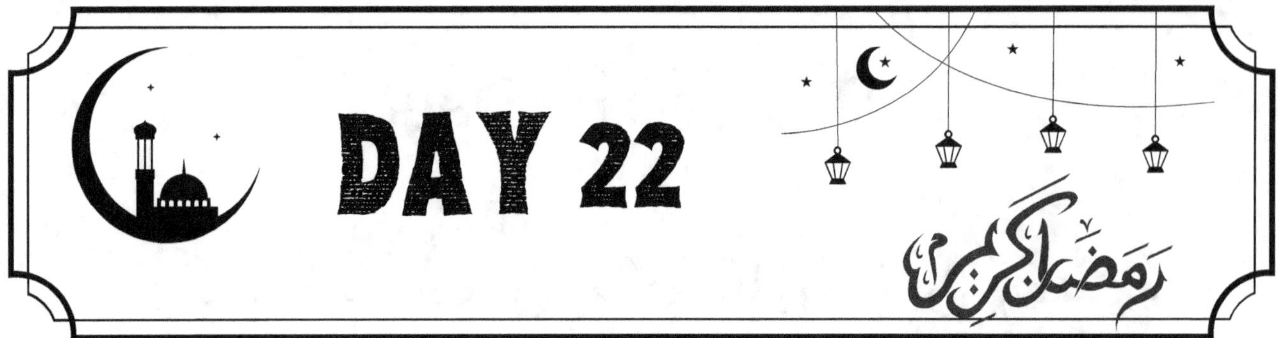

color a flag for every prayer you made

FAJR	ZUHR	ASR	MAGHRIB	ISHA
2	4	4	3	4

My goal for to day

....
....
....

choosenan ayah to copy here

بِسْمِ اللهِ الرَّحْمَٰنِ الرَّحِيمِ

Healthy Habits

WATER:

EXERCISE: _ _ _ _ _ _ _ _ _ _

MOOD:

My good dees

I read quran ☐

I did zikr ☐

I gavr sadaqah ☐

Dua of The Day

رَبَّنَا آمَنَّا فَاغْفِرْ لَنَا وَارْحَمْنَا وَأَنتَ خَيْرُ الرَّاحِمِينَ

RABBANA AMANNA FAGHFIR LANA WARHAMNA WA ANTA KHAIRUR RAHIMIIN

"OUR LORD, WE HAVE BELIEVED, SO FORGIVE US AND HAVE MERCY UPON US, AND YOU ARE THE BEST OF THE MERCIFUL."
– 23:109 –

Reflections of The Day

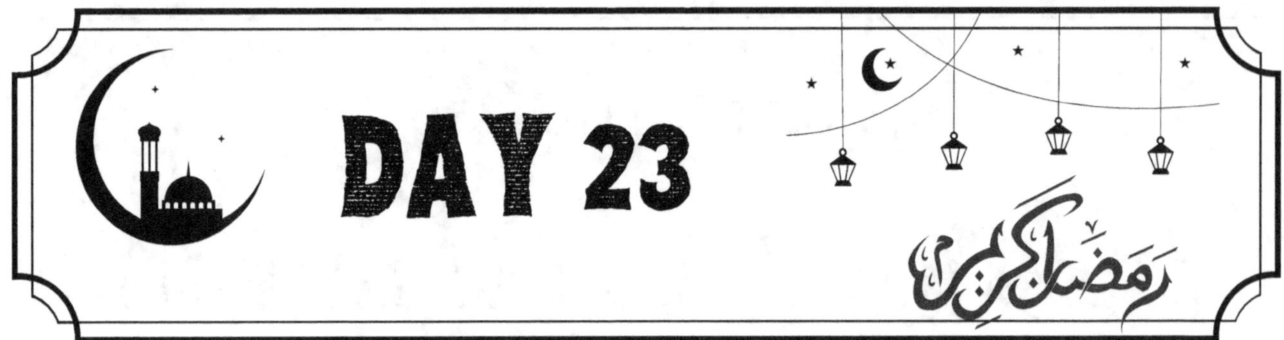

color a flag for every prayer you made

FAJR	ZUHR	ASR	MAGHRIB	ISHA
2	4	4	3	4

My goal for to day

....

....

....

Healthy Habits

WATER:

EXERCISE: _ _ _ _ _ _ _ _ _ _

MOOD:

My good dees

I read quran ☐

I did zikr ☐

I gavr sadaqah ☐

choosenan ayah to copy here

بِسْمِ اللَّهِ الرَّحْمَٰنِ الرَّحِيمِ

....

....

....

....

....

....

Dua of The Day

رَبَّنَا هَبْ لَنَا مِنْ أَزْوَاجِنَا وَذُرِّيَّاتِنَا قُرَّةَ أَعْيُنٍ وَاجْعَلْنَا لِلْمُتَّقِينَ إِمَامًا

RABBANA HABLANA MIN AZWAAJINA WADHURRIY-YATINA, QURRATA 'AYIONI WA-JALNA LIL-MUTTAQEENA IMAAMA

"OUR LORD, GRANT US FROM AMONG OUR WIVES AND OFFSPRING COMFORT TO OUR EYES AND MAKE US A LEADER [I.E., EXAMPLE] FOR THE RIGHTEOUS."

– 25:74 –

Reflections of The Day

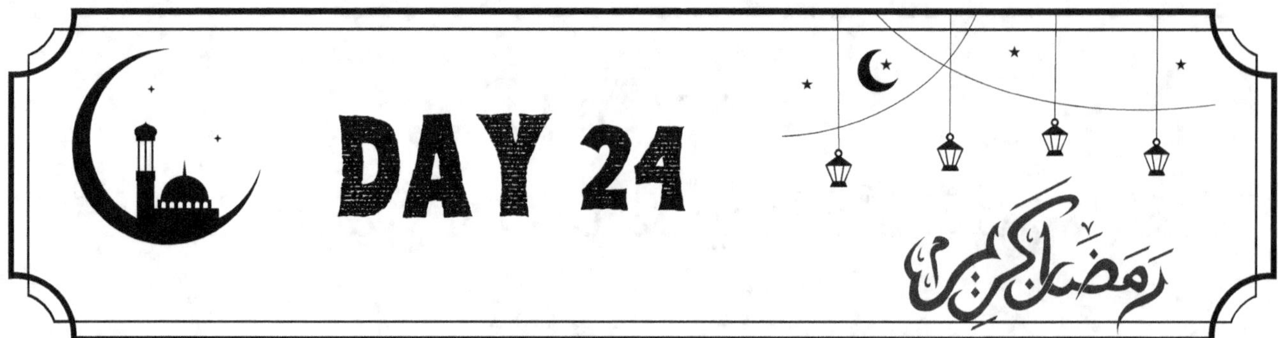

color a flag for every prayer you made

FAJR	ZUHR	ASR	MAGHRIB	ISHA
2	4	4	3	4

My goal for to day

....

....

....

Healthy Habits

WATER:

EXERCISE: _ _ _ _ _ _ _ _ _ _

MOOD:

My good dees

I read quran ☐

I did zikr ☐

I gavr sadaqah ☐

choosenan ayah to copy here

بِسْمِ اللهِ الرَّحْمَنِ الرَّحِيمِ

....

....

....

....

....

....

Dua of The Day

رَبَّنَا لَغَفُورٌ شَكُورٌ

RABBANA LA GHAFURUN SHAKUR

"OUR LORD IS FORGIVING AND APPRECIATIVE"
– 35:34 –

Reflections of The Day

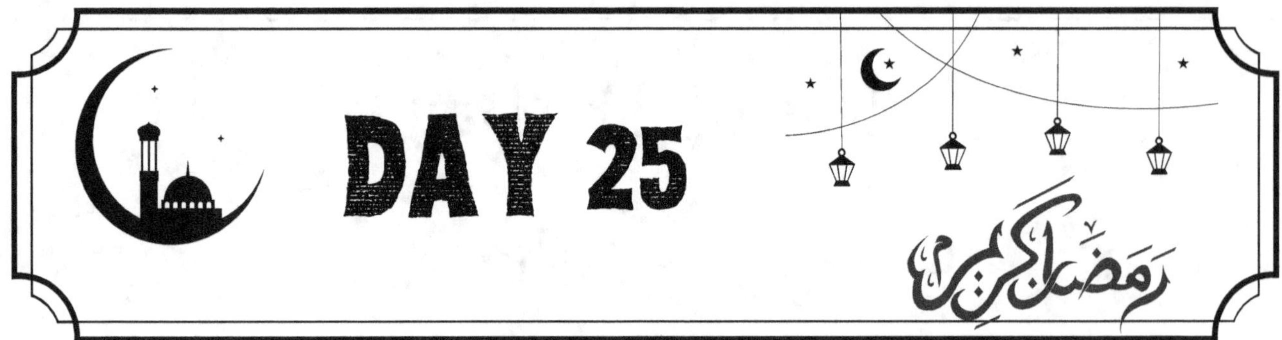

DAY 25

color a flag for every prayer you made

FAJR	ZUHR	ASR	MAGHRIB	ISHA
2	4	4	3	4

My goal for to day

....

....

....

Healthy Habits

WATER:

EXERCISE: _ _ _ _ _ _ _ _ _ _

MOOD:

My good dees

I read quran ☐

I did zikr ☐

I gavr sadaqah ☐

choosenan ayah to copy here

بِسْمِ اللّٰهِ الرَّحْمٰنِ الرَّحِيمِ

....

....

....

....

....

....

Dua of The Day

رَبَّنَا إِنَّكَ رَؤُوفٌ رَّحِيمٌ

RABBANA INNAKA RA'UFUR RAHIM

"OUR LORD, INDEED YOU ARE KIND AND MERCIFUL."
– 59:10 –

Reflections of The Day

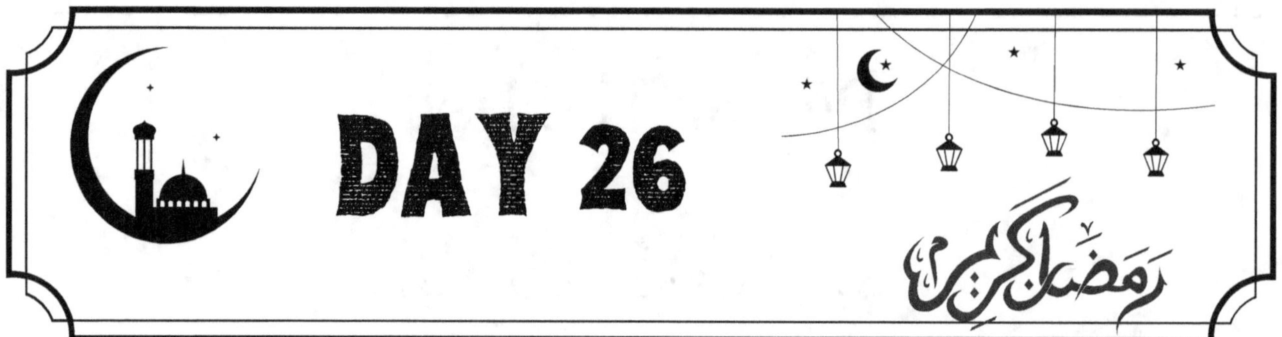

color a flag for every prayer you made

FAJR	ZUHR	ASR	MAGHRIB	ISHA
2	4	4	3	4

My goal for to day

choosenan ayah to copy here

بِسْمِ اللهِ الرَّحْمَنِ الرَّحِيمِ

Healthy Habits

WATER:

EXERCISE: _ _ _ _ _ _ _ _ _ _

MOOD:

My good dees

I read quran ☐

I did zikr ☐

I gavr sadaqah ☐

Dua of The Day

رَّبَّنَا عَلَيْكَ تَوَكَّلْنَا وَإِلَيْكَ أَنَبْنَا وَإِلَيْكَ الْمَصِيرُ

RABBANA 'ALAIKA TAWAKKALNA WA-ILAIKA ANABNA WA-ILAIKAL MASIR

"OUR LORD, UPON YOU WE HAVE RELIED, AND TO YOU WE HAVE RETURNED, AND TO YOU IS THE DESTINATION."
– 60:4 –

Reflections of The Day

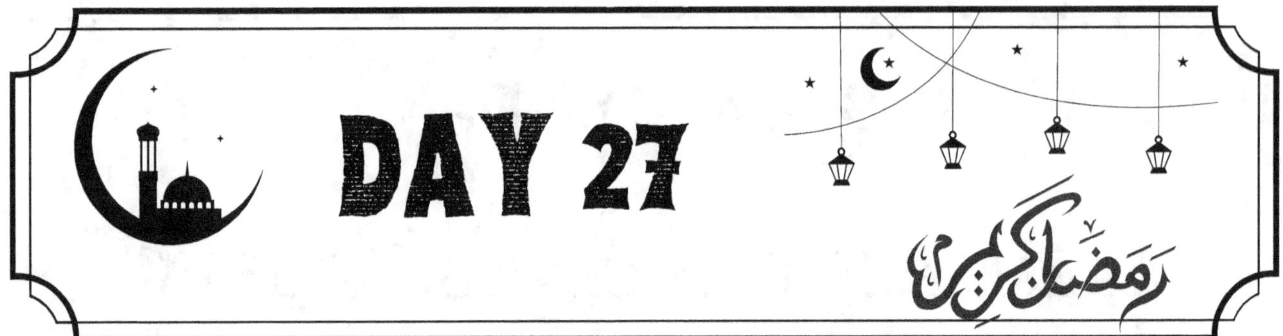

color a flag for every prayer you made

FAJR	ZUHR	ASR	MAGHRIB	ISHA
2	4	4	3	4

My goal for to day

....

....

....

Healthy Habits

WATER:

EXERCISE: _ _ _ _ _ _ _ _ _ _

MOOD:

My good dees

I read quran ☐

I did zikr ☐

I gavr sadaqah ☐

choosenan ayah to copy here

بِسْمِ اللَّهِ الرَّحْمَٰنِ الرَّحِيمِ

Dua of The Day

رَبَّنَا لَا تَجْعَلْنَا فِتْنَةً لِّلَّذِينَ كَفَرُوا وَاغْفِرْ لَنَا رَبَّنَا إِنَّكَ أَنتَ الْعَزِيزُ الْحَكِيمُ

RABBANA LA TAJ'ALNA FITNATAL LILLADHINA KAFARU WAGHFIR LANA
RABBANA INNAKA ANTAL 'AZEEZUL-HAKEEM

"OUR LORD, MAKE US NOT [OBJECTS OF] TORMENT FOR THE
DISBELIEVERS AND FORGIVE US, OUR LORD. INDEED, IT IS YOU WHO IS
THE EXALTED IN MIGHT, THE WISE."
– 60:5 –

Reflections of The Day

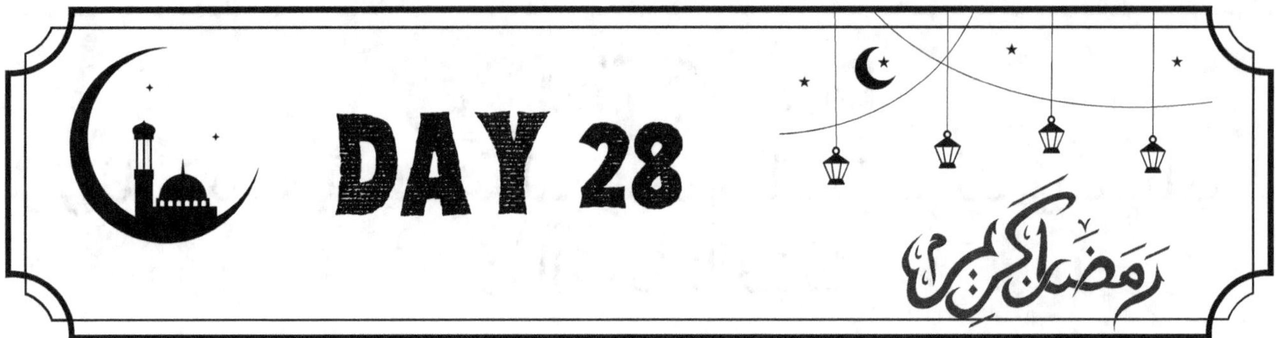

color a flag for every prayer you made

FAJR	ZUHR	ASR	MAGHRIB	ISHA
2	4	4	3	4

My goal for to day

....
....
....

choosenan ayah to copy here

بِسْمِ اللهِ الرَّحْمٰنِ الرَّحِيْمِ

....
....
....
....
....
....

Healthy Habits

WATER:

EXERCISE: _ _ _ _ _ _ _ _ _ _

MOOD:

My good dees

I read quran ☐

I did zikr ☐

I gavr sadaqah ☐

Dua of The Day

رَبَّنَا أَتْمِمْ لَنَا نُورَنَا وَاغْفِرْ لَنَا إِنَّكَ عَلَى كُلِّ شَيْءٍ قَدِيرٌ

RABBANA ATMIM LANA NURANA WAIGHFIR LANA INNAKA 'ALA KULLI SHAI-IN QADIR

"OUR LORD, PERFECT FOR US OUR LIGHT AND FORGIVE US. INDEED, YOU ARE OVER ALL THINGS COMPETENT."
– 66:8 –

Reflections of The Day

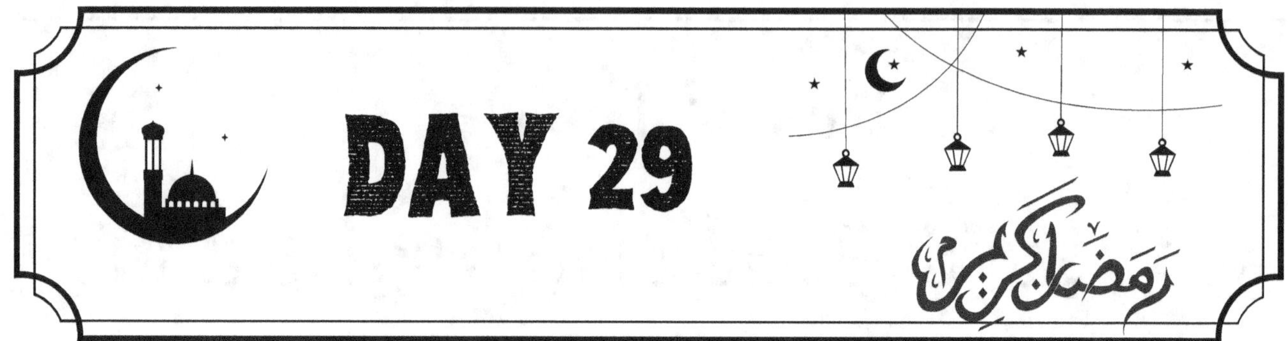

color a flag for every prayer you made

FAJR	ZUHR	ASR	MAGHRIB	ISHA
2	4	4	3	4

My goal for to day

....

....

....

Healthy Habits

WATER:

EXERCISE: _ _ _ _ _ _ _ _ _ _

MOOD:

My good dees

I read quran ☐

I did zikr ☐

I gavr sadaqah ☐

choosenan ayah to copy here

Dua of The Day

رَبَّنَا وَسِعْتَ كُلَّ شَيْءٍ رَّحْمَةً وَعِلْمًا فَاغْفِرْ لِلَّذِينَ تَابُوا وَاتَّبَعُوا سَبِيلَكَ وَقِهِمْ عَذَابَ الْجَحِيمِ

RABBANA WASI'TA KULLA SHA'IR RAHMATAN WA 'ILMAN FAGHFIR LILLADHINA TABU WATTABA'U SABILAKA WAQIHIM 'ADHABAL-JAHIIM

"OUR LORD, YOU HAVE ENCOMPASSED ALL THINGS IN MERCY AND KNOWLEDGE, SO FORGIVE THOSE WHO HAVE REPENTED AND FOLLOWED YOUR WAY AND PROTECT THEM FROM THE PUNISHMENT OF HELLFIRE."

– 40:7 –

Reflections of The Day

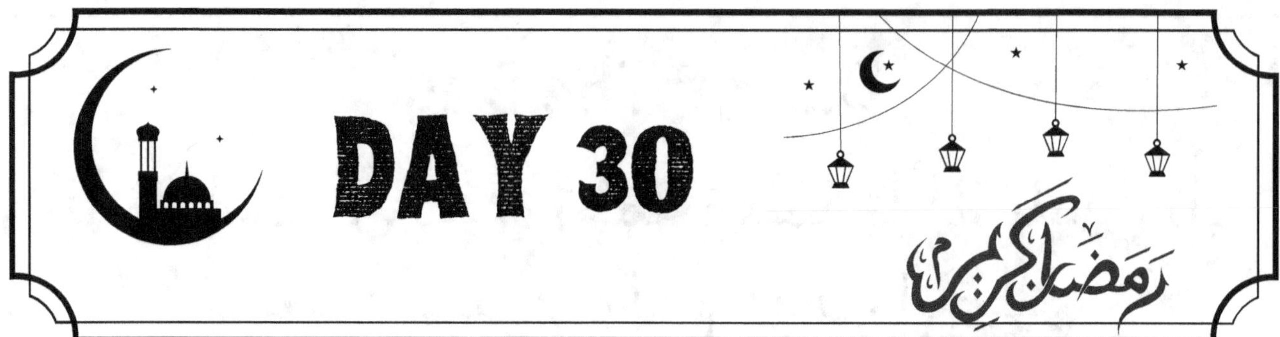

color a flag for every prayer you made

FAJR	ZUHR	ASR	MAGHRIB	ISHA
2	4	4	3	4

My goal for to day

....

....

....

choosenan ayah to copy here

بِسْمِ اللَّهِ الرَّحْمَٰنِ الرَّحِيمِ

Healthy Habits

WATER:

EXERCISE: _ _ _ _ _ _ _ _ _ _ _

MOOD:

My good dees

I read quran ☐

I did zikr ☐

I gavr sadaqah ☐

Dua of The Day

اللَّهُمَّ إِنَّكَ عَفُوٌّ تُحِبُّ الْعَفْوَ فَاعْفُ عَنِّي

**ALLAHUMMA INNAKA AFUWWUN
TUHIBBUL AFWA FA'FU ANNEE**

Reflections of The Day

9 798416 831875